RISING STARS ASSESSMENT

English Progress Tests

Year 1

Helen Betts

Series Advisors: Cornwall Learning

RISING STARS

CORNWALL LEARNING

Rising Stars UK Ltd, 7 Hatchers Mews, Bermondsey Street, London SE1 3GS

www.risingstars-uk.com

First published 2014
Reprinted 2014 (four times), 2015 (five times)

Text, design and layout © Rising Stars UK Ltd 2014

Reading Tests and Autumn 1, Autumn 2 and Spring 1 Grammar Tests based on material originally written by
Kate Ruttle, © Rising Stars UK Ltd 2010

All facts were correct at time of going to press. All referenced websites were correct at the time this book went to press.

The right of Helen Betts to be identified as the author of this work has been asserted by her in accordance with the
Copyright, Design and Patents Act 1998.

Author: Helen Betts
Educational consultants: Shareen Mayers, Sutton Improvement and Support Services, and Sara Moult, Cornwall Learning
Series editor: Maddy Barnes
Accessibility reviewer: Vivien Kilburn
Editorial: Lesley Densham-Wilson for Green Desert Ltd and Sarah Davies
Design: Andy Wilson for Green Desert Ltd
Illustrations: David Woodroffe
Cover design: Burville-Riley Partnership

Rising Stars is grateful to the following people and schools who contributed to the development of these materials:
Plumcroft Primary School, London; St Helens Teaching Schools Alliance; St Nicholas CE Primary School, Chislehurst;
St Margaret's CE Primary School, Heywood, Rochdale; Tennyson Road Primary School, Luton

All rights reserved. No part of this publication may be reproduced, stored in a retrieval system, or transmitted,
in any form by any means, electronic, mechanical, photocopying, recording or otherwise, without the prior
permission of Rising Stars.

British Library Cataloguing in Publication Data.
A CIP record for this book is available from the British Library.
ISBN: 978 1 78339 096 0

Printed by Ashford Colour Press

Contents

	Page
Introduction	4
My progress sheet	8

Reading tests
Autumn test 1: Fiction	9
Autumn test 2: Non-fiction	12
Spring test 1: Fiction	15
Spring test 2: Non-fiction	18
Summer test 1: Fiction	21
Summer test 2: Non-fiction	24

Grammar, punctuation and vocabulary tests
Autumn test 1	27
Autumn test 2	30
Spring test 1	32
Spring test 2	34
Summer test 1	37
Summer test 2	40

Spelling tests
Spring test 2	43
Summer test 1	46
Summer test 2	49

Answers and mark schemes
Reading tests	52
Grammar, punctuation and vocabulary tests	56
Coverage grid: Reading	61
Coverage grid: Grammar, punctuation and vocabulary	63

Introduction

Why use Rising Stars Assessment Progress Tests?

The *Rising Stars Assessment English Progress Tests* have been developed to support teachers assess the progress their pupils are making against the requirements of the 2014 National Curriculum Programme of Study for English in Year 1. They include tests for reading, for grammar, punctuation and vocabulary and for spelling. All *Rising Stars Assessment English Progress Tests* are designed to support effective classroom assessment and are easy to use and mark.

The *Rising Stars Assessment English Progress Tests* include half-termly tests for reading and for grammar, punctuation and vocabulary. There are also half-termly tests for spelling from the second half of the spring term. All the tests have been:

- written by primary English assessment specialists
- reviewed by primary English curriculum and assessment experts.

How do the tests track progress?

The results data from the tests can be used to track progress. They show whether pupils are making the expected progress for their year, more than expected progress or less than expected progress. This data can then be used alongside other evidence to enable effective planning of future teaching and learning, for reporting to parents and as evidence for Ofsted inspections. If teachers are using the CD-ROM version of the tests, the results data can be keyed into the Progress Tracker (see pages 6–7 for more information) which automatically shows the progress of individual pupils against the Programme of Study and the results for all pupils by question and test. Marks are also captured by assessment focus (AF) for the reading tests, and for G, P, V and S for the grammar, punctuation and vocabulary tests. Data can also be exported into the school' management information system (MIS).

About the *English Progress Tests*

The tests are written to cover the requirements of the Programme of Study for the 2014 Nationa Curriculum including the Appendices for English. There are separate tests for reading and grammar, punctuation and vocabulary for each half term and for spelling from the second half c the spring term. The number of marks for each test is as follows:

Test	Marks
Reading	10
Grammar, punctuation and vocabulary	10
Spelling	10

The first reading test for each half term has questions based on a fiction extract; the second uses a non-fiction extract. The extracts used in the tests are age-appropriate ones. The reading tests assess across a range of skills as exemplified by the assessment focuses for reading. The assessment focuses covered in the Year 1 tests are:

AF1: use a range of strategies, including accurate decoding of text, to read for meaning;

AF2: understand, describe, select or retrieve information, events or ideas from texts and use quotation and reference to text;

AF3: deduce, infer or interpret information, events or ideas from texts.

From 2016 the national tests will use strands instead of assessment focuses. Full details of which AF and strand each question assesses can be found in the Reading tests Coverage grid on page 61.

Questions in the grammar, punctuation and vocabulary tests use the cognitive domains of knowledge and comprehension derived from Bloom's taxonomy. Each question in the grammar, punctuation and vocabulary tests is marked G (grammar), P (punctuation) or V (vocabulary and language strategies). A few questions in tests taken earlier in the year are marked S (spelling). These questions are Reception-level questions and assess skills leading into the National Curriculum requirements. Further details of what the questions cover can be found in the Grammar, punctuation and vocabulary tests Coverage grid on page 63.

Spellings are assessed using pictures with labels (spring term) and short contextualised sentences (summer term). Spelling tests are provided from the second half of the spring term to give pupils time to develop and secure their phonic knowledge in the first part of Year 1.

Test demand

Test demand increases both within tests and across the year, which means that tests at the beginning of the year are easier than those at the end of the year.

Tracking progress

The marks pupils score in the tests can be used to track how they are progressing against the expected outcomes for their year group. The marks for each test have been split into three progress zones:

- less than expected progress
- expected progress
- more than expected progress

The zones for the Year 1 English tests are as follows:

Zone mark range		
Less than expected progress	Expected progress	More than expected progress
0–5	6–8	9–10

The table gives the mark ranges for the progress zones for each test which you can use to see how well each pupil is doing in each test. If pupils are making the expected progress for their year they will be consistently scoring marks in the middle zone of marks in the tests. The higher the mark in the zone, the more secure you can be that they are making expected progress.

How to use the *English Progress Tests*

Preparation and timings

1. Make enough copies of the test(s) for each pupil to have their own copy.
2. Hand out the papers and ensure pupils are seated appropriately so that they can't see each other's papers.

Introduction

3 Pupils will need pens or pencils and erasers. Encourage pupils to cross out answers rather than rub them out.
4 There are no time limits for the tests but normal practice is to allow a minute per mark for written tests. Teachers may however prefer to administer the tests in chunks for younger pupils and to allow breaks.

Supporting pupils during the tests

Before the test explain to the pupils that the test is an opportunity to show what they know, understand and can do. They should try to answer all the questions but should not worry if there are some they can't do.

Many pupils will be able to work independently in the tests, with minimal support from the teacher or a teaching assistant. However pupils should be encouraged to 'have a go' at a question, or to move on to a fresh question if they appear to be stuck, to ensure that no pupil becomes distressed.

It is important that pupils receive appropriate support, but are not unfairly advantaged or disadvantaged. For example, given the age of the pupils teachers may wish to read out the questions for the grammar, punctuation and vocabulary tests as the aim is to assess grammar, punctuation and vocabulary skills rather than reading in these tests.

Teachers could also consider using the version of the test on the CD-ROM and projecting it onto a whiteboard to support a whole class or group to take the tests. You may choose to refer to the words on the whiteboard and read them aloud so that pupils can follow them on the screen and on their own test paper and then write their answers on their papers individually.

Marking the tests

Use the detailed mark scheme and your professional judgement to award marks. Do not award half marks.

Feeding back to pupils

Once the test has been marked, use a five-minute feedback session with the pupils to help them review their answers. Wherever possible pupils should be encouraged to make their own corrections as in this way they will become more aware of their own strengths and weaknesses. A template 'My progress' sheet is provided on page 8 to help with this. Encourage pupils to colour the face which best shows how well they think they did in the test (there are three faces to choose from – one happy, one sad and one neutral). They should then add the number of the question that they found most difficult. Finally, pupils should fill in the speech bubble to indicate what they need more help with. Some pupils will be able to do this by themselves but some may find a word bank supplied by the teacher useful. The teacher or another adult may need to act as scribe for some pupils.

Using the Progress Tracker

The table on page 5 gives the mark ranges for the progress zones for each test which you can use to see how well each pupil is doing in each test. If pupils are making the expected progress for their year they will be consistently scoring marks in the middle zone of marks in the tests.

The higher the mark in the zone, the more secure you can be that they are making expected progress.

The CD-ROM version of the *English Progress Tests* includes an interactive Progress Tracker, which allows you to enter the marks for each question for each test by pupil. This then automatically shows you which zone the pupil is in and also the zone distribution for the class so that you can track the progress of individual pupils and the whole class.

The Progress Tracker also enables you to review the marks for each question so that you can identify areas where some or all pupils may need further support and areas where some or all pupils are ready to be stretched further. It also provides a separate summary of marks for each pupil for the assessment focuses (AFs) for the reading tests and for G, P, V and S for the grammar, punctuation and vocabulary tests so that you can identify if pupils have strengths or weaknesses in a particular skill. Questions in the reading tests are mapped to the *Rising Stars Progression Framework for Reading*. Questions in the grammar, punctuation and vocabulary tests are mapped to the National Curriculum Programme of Study for English. The mapped statements can be viewed by rolling over the codes below the question numbers.

If required, data from the tests can be exported into the school's management information system (MIS) so that it can be used alongside other data in whole school monitoring including the monitoring of specific groups of pupils, such as Pupil Premium.

Full details about the Progress Tracker are provided on the CD-ROM.

My progress

Name: _____ Class: _____ Date: _____

Test: _____

★ How well did you do?

★ Which question did you find the hardest?

★ What do you need more help with?

Year 1 Reading: Autumn test 1: Fiction

Sam was sad. His pet cat was ill. It had a bad leg.

1

Sam and the cat went to the vet. The vet said, "A dog bit the cat's leg and now the leg hurts. It will get better."

2

Year 1   *Reading: Autumn test 1: Fiction*

| Name: | Class: | Date: |

✓ one.

1) The pet is a

☐   ☐   ☐

AF1
1 mark

2) It had a bad

☐   ☐   ☐

AF1
1 mark

3) It went to the

☐   ☐   ☐

AF1
1 mark

✓ one.

4) A _____ bit the cat's leg.

rat ☐   dog ☐   hen ☐

AF2
1 mark

5) Sam was _____.

wet ☐   sad ☐   bad ☐

AF2
1 mark

/ 5
Total for this page

✓ **yes** or **no**.

6 The cat is Sam's pet.

yes ☐   no ☐

7 The cat bit a dog's leg.

yes ☐   no ☐

8 The cat's leg hurts.

yes ☐   no ☐

9 The vet was sad.

yes ☐   no ☐

10 The leg will get better.

yes ☐   no ☐

Some pets

a dog

a fish

a bird

a cat

a rabbit

a hamster

This is Tess. Tess likes pets. She is a vet.

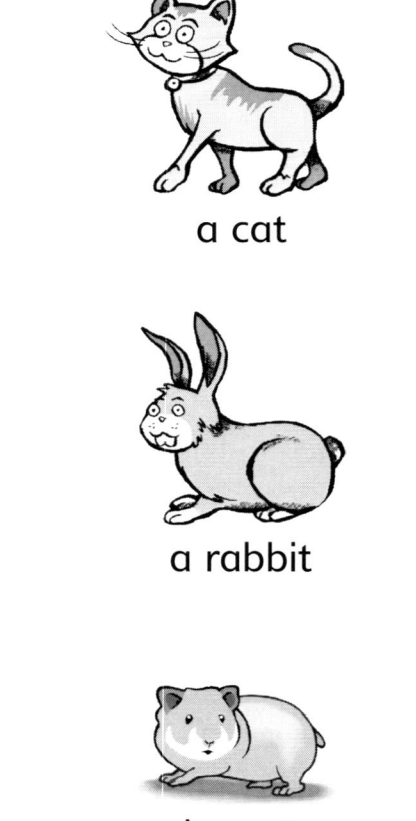

You can take a pet to see the vet.
The vet can help a pet if it is hurt.

Year 1   Reading: Autumn test 2: Non-fiction

Name:	Class:	Date:

Draw lines to match.

1. 🐱

2. 🐹   bird

3. 🐦   cat

          hamster

✓ one.

4. Tess is a _____.

   pet ☐   vet ☐   fish ☐

5. Tess likes _____.

   pits ☐   pets ☐   pots ☐

Year 1   Reading: Autumn test 2: Non-fiction

✓ **yes** or **no**.

6 Tess helps vets.

yes ☐   no ☐

7 A cat is a pet.

yes ☐   no ☐

8 A hamster is a pet.

yes ☐   no ☐

9 Tess is hurt.

yes ☐   no ☐

10 You can take a pet to see the vet.

yes ☐   no ☐

Max saw a cat in the park. The cat was thin.

Max said, "Mum, can I give the cat some food?"
"Yes you can," said Mum.

Max fed the cat. He gave it a bowl of food.

The cat ate all the food. Now it is fat!

Year 1   Reading: Spring test 1: Fiction

| Name: | Class: | Date: |

✓ one.

1   Max saw a

☐   ☐   ☐

AF1
1 mark

✓ one.

2   The cat was _____ .

fat ☐   sad ☐   thin ☐

AF2
1 mark

3   Max gave the cat _____ .

Mum ☐   food ☐   yes ☐

AF2
1 mark

4   The cat _____ the food.

went ☐   thin ☐   ate ☐

AF2
1 mark

5   Now the cat is _____ .

fat ☐   sad ☐   thin ☐

AF2
1 mark

/ 5
Total for this page

© Rising Stars UK Ltd 2014   *You may photocopy this page*

✓ **yes** or **no**.

6) The cat was in the park.

yes ☐   no ☐

7) Max gave the cat to the dog.

yes ☐   no ☐

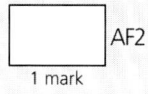

8) The cat ate a bowl of food.

yes ☐   no ☐

9) Max fed the fish every day.

yes ☐   no ☐

10) Mum fed the cat.

yes ☐   no ☐

Pets

Cats

Cats are good pets.

You must feed a cat every day.

Cats need water too.

Fish

Fish are good pets.
They live in a tank.

You must feed a fish every week.
Fish eat dry fish food.

This is fish food.

This fish likes to play in the weeds.

The fish can eat the weeds too.

Year 1   Reading: Spring test 2: Non-fiction

Name:	Class:	Date:

Draw **one** line to match the picture to the right words.

1.

This is fish food.

This is a cat.

This is a tin of cat food.

AF1
1 mark

✓ one.

2. This is a

rabbit ☐   cat ☐   fish ☐

AF1
1 mark

3. This is a

dog ☐   cat ☐   can ☐

AF1
1 mark

4. Pet fish live in a _____.

tin ☐   tank ☐   box ☐

AF2
1 mark

5. Fish play in the _____.

tin ☐   weeds ☐   food ☐

AF2
1 mark

/ 5
Total for this page

✓ **yes** or **no**.

6 You must feed a cat every day.

yes ☐ no ☐

AF2
1 mark

7 You must feed a fish every week.

yes ☐ no ☐

AF2
1 mark

8 Cats need water.

yes ☐ no ☐

AF2
1 mark

9 Fish eat cat food.

yes ☐ no ☐

AF2
1 mark

10 Can a fish eat weeds?

yes ☐ no ☐

AF2
1 mark

/ 10
Total for this test

Year 1   Reading: Summer test 1: Fiction

Sam lives on a farm. His dad is a farmer. Sam's dad asks Sam to help him on the farm.

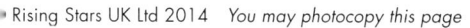

Sam and Mop are sad. They want to play in the mud.

Sam has to get some grass for Mop.

1

Then he gets the eggs.

Next he gets the logs.

Sam washes the tractor. It is hard work!

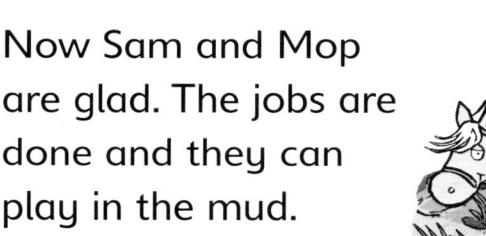

Now Sam and Mop are glad. The jobs are done and they can play in the mud.

2

Year 1   *Reading: Summer test 1: Fiction*

Name:	Class:	Date:

✓ one.

1 Mop is a

☐ tractor   ☐ horse   ☐ dad

AF1 — 1 mark

✓ one.

2 Sam lives on a _____.

boat ☐   farm ☐   tractor ☐

AF2 — 1 mark

3 Sam's dad needs some _____.

hay ☐   hope ☐   help ☐

AF2 — 1 mark

4 Sam and Mop want to play in the _____.

sand ☐   snow ☐   mud ☐

AF2 — 1 mark

5 Sam has to get some _____.

sand ☐   grass ☐   mud ☐

AF2 — 1 mark

/ 5
Total for this page

22   © Rising Stars UK Ltd 2014   *You may photocopy this page*

✓ **yes** or **no**.

6) Sam gets the eggs and the logs.

yes ☐   no ☐

7) Washing the tractor is easy.

yes ☐   no ☐

8) At the end, Sam and Mop are happy.

yes ☐   no ☐

Answer the questions.

9) **At first**, why are Sam and Mop sad?

_____

_____

10) **At the end**, why can Sam and Mop play in the mud?

_____

_____

Swimming

Do you like going swimming? You can have lots of fun playing in the water!

You will need:

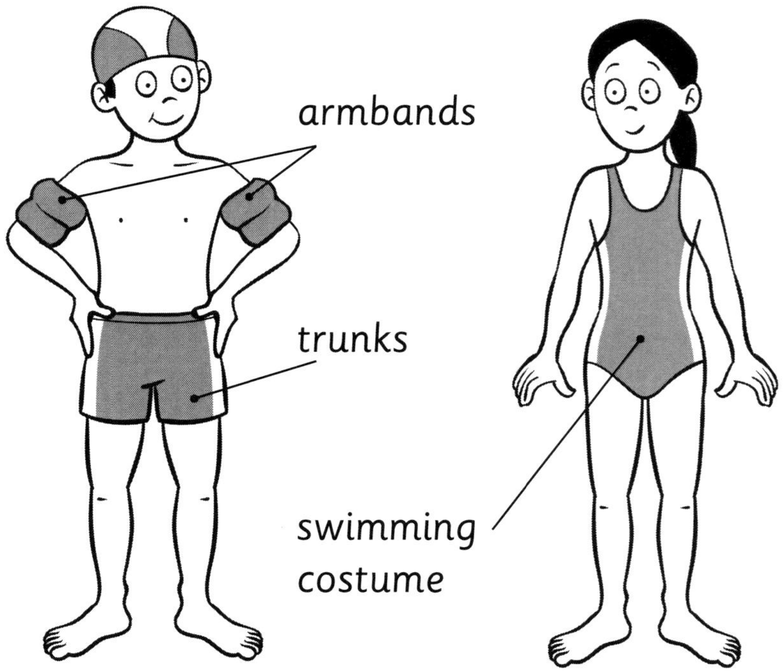

- armbands
- trunks
- swimming costume

At the swimming pool

Swimming is fun but you need to stay safe. Here are some rules you must follow.

- Stay with Mum or Dad. Do not go in the pool on your own.  
- Walk at the side of the pool. Do not run or you might slip. 
- Do not jump into the pool. You might hurt another person.

Have fun!

Year 1   Reading: Summer test 2: Non-fiction

| Name: | Class: | Date: |

✓ to show whether each is **something you need** or a **rule**.
One has been done for you.

	something you need	a rule
armbands	✓	
1 Stay with Mum or Dad.		
2 swimming costume		

AF2
2 marks

✓ one.

3 You will need some _____.

    trousers ☐   trunks ☐   tables ☐

AF2
1 mark

4 You must follow the rules to stay _____.

    still ☐   happy ☐   safe ☐

AF2
1 mark

5 Stay with Mum or Dad at the _____.

    beach ☐   pool ☐   shop ☐

AF2
1 mark

/ 5
Total for this page

Rising Stars UK Ltd 2014   *You may photocopy this page*

Year 1   Reading: Summer test 2: Non-fiction

✓ **yes** or **no**.

6 You can jump into the pool.

　　　　yes ☐   no ☐

7 Playing in the water can be fun.

　　　　yes ☐   no ☐

8 You can go in the water on your own.

　　　　yes ☐   no ☐

Answer the questions.

9 What might happen if you run at the pool?

_____

_____

10 Why can't you jump into the pool?

_____

_____

Year 1   Grammar, punctuation and vocabulary: Autumn test 1

| Name: | Class: | Date: |

1) Circle **two** pictures that begin with the same sound.

☐ 1 mark

2) Circle **two** pictures that begin with the sound **m**.

☐ 1 mark

3) Circle **two** pictures that rhyme.

☐ 1 mark

/ 3
Total for this page

Year 1   *Grammar, punctuation and vocabulary: Autumn test 1*

Look at each picture. Circle the correct word.

4   tin   sun   dog

5   hat   hen   hum

6   pin   pit   pot

Year 1   Grammar, punctuation and vocabulary: Autumn test 1

Finish each sentence. Circle the correct word.

7 It _____ a hot day.

        at   you   was

8 It is _____ the box.

        is   it   in

9 I _____ my mum.

        at   like   he

10 This is _____ red fish.

        the   we   it

/ 10
Total for this test

Year 1   *Grammar, punctuation and vocabulary: Autumn test 2*

Name:	Class:	Date:

Practice question

What letter does this **begin** with?

(c)   m   p

1. What letter does this **begin** with?

   c   t   s

2. What letters does this **begin** with?

   ch   sh   th

3. Look at the picture. Circle the correct word.

   sun   dig   hat

4. Look at the picture. Circle the correct word.

   dot   bed   kid

5. Look at the picture. Circle the correct word.

   tip   tap   tan

Year 1   Grammar, punctuation and vocabulary: Autumn test 2

Finish each sentence. Circle the correct word.

6) This is _____ mum.

          it   my   at

1 mark G

7) Can _____ see it?

          you   get   big

1 mark G

8) I am _____ to the shop.

          go   get   going

1 mark G

9) I _____ that frog.

          look   like   leg

1 mark G

10) Can you _____ him?

          grin   grab   gran

1 mark G

/ 10
Total for this test

Year 1 Grammar, punctuation and vocabulary: Spring test 1

Name: Class: Date:

Practice question

What letter does this **begin** with?

(c)   h   d

1) What letter does this **begin** with?

b   m   d

2) Look at the picture. Circle the correct word.

fox   bus   hop

3) Look at the picture. Circle the correct word.

zip   win   six

4) Look at the picture. Circle the correct word.

fog   frog   flag

5) Look at the picture. Circle the correct word.

ship   fin   fish

Year 1   Grammar, punctuation and vocabulary: Spring test 1

Finish each sentence. Circle the correct word to fill the gap.

6) It _____ a hen.

        up   is   this

G 1 mark

7) I am _____ away.

        going   got   good

G 1 mark

8) I _____ a big egg.

        help   have   him

G 1 mark

9) This is my _____.

        house   made   was

G 1 mark

10) Did you _____ a cake?

        some   your   make

G 1 mark

/ 10
Total for this test

© Rising Stars UK Ltd 2014   *You may photocopy this page*

Year 1   Grammar, punctuation and vocabulary: Spring test 2

| Name: | Class: | Date: |

1 Match the lower case letters with the capital letters.
One has been done for you.

lower case letter   capital letter

b —————————— R
e   N
n   B
r   E

2 **Plural** means **more than one**.
Which of these words are plural? Circle **two** words.

frogs   train   spoon   boys   table

3 Which of these is a question? ✓ **one**.

I have a pet rabbit. ☐

Who is that? ☐

My name is Max. ☐

4 Finish the sentence using these words. Draw lines from the words to the correct spaces.
Use each word **once**.

(red)   (is)   (hat)

My _____ _____ _____ .

5 Draw **one** line to show which word can have **un-** added to the beginning.

un-   nice
       see
       kind

6 **Plural** means **more than one**.
Add **one** letter at the end of each word to make it plural.

car___   dog___

7 Circle **one** word to complete the sentence.

buzzing   buzzed   buzz

The bee was _____ around his face.

8 Look at this sentence. Circle **one** word that should begin with a capital letter.

Every weekend, james goes swimming.

☐ P
1 mark

9 Look at this question.

What time is it?

Write another question of your own that begins with *What*.

What _____

_____?

☐ G
1 mark

10 Look at this picture.

Write **one** sentence about the picture.

_____

_____.

☐ G
1 mark

☐ /10
Total for this test

Year 1   Grammar, punctuation and vocabulary: Summer test 1

| Name: | Class: | Date: |

1 Circle **one** word to complete the sentence.

fast   faster   fastest

I can run _____ than you.

V
1 mark

2 Look at the label for this picture.

one dish

Write **one** word to finish the labels below.

one _____

one _____

G
1 mark

3 Which of these is a sentence? ✓ **one**.

Look at all the   ☐
Then he ran to   ☐
She has a green coat. ☐

G
1 mark

/ 3
Total for this page

Year 1   Grammar, punctuation and vocabulary: Summer test 1

4 Draw **one** line to show which sentence should finish with an exclamation mark (!).

Come back

The flower is yellow   !

It is raining

P
1 mark

5 Which of these sentences is missing the word *and*?
✓ **one**.

and

He went to _____ park. ☐

I love my _____ shoes. ☐

It was windy _____ cold. ☐

G
1 mark

6 Write a sentence using these words.
Use each word **once**.

a   Tim   fish
had   pet

_____.

G
1 mark

/3
Total for this page

Year 1   Grammar, punctuation and vocabulary: Summer test 1

7 ✓ **one** word to finish the sentence.

boat ☐   boates ☐   boats ☐

I saw two _____ sail by.

G
1 mark

8 Which of these words can have **un-** added to the beginning? ✓ **two**.

give ☐   fair ☐   happy ☐   play ☐

V
1 mark

9 Write **one** sentence about yourself, beginning with **I**.

I _____

_____

G
1 mark

10 Look at this sentence. There is **one** mistake.
Copy out the sentence and correct the mistake.

On friday I went to the park.

_____

_____ .

P
1 mark

/10
Total for this test

© Rising Stars UK Ltd 2014   *You may photocopy this page*   39

Year 1   *Grammar, punctuation and vocabulary: Summer test 2*

| Name: | Class: | Date: |

1 Look at this picture.

Write **one** word in each space to describe the monster.

The monster is _____ and

_____.

G 1 mark

2 Circle **one** word to finish the sentence.

tall   taller   tallest

Anna is the _____ in her class.

V 1 mark

3 Look at this question.

Why do dogs bark?

Write another question of your own that begins with **Why**.

Why _____

G 1 mark

4 **Plural** means **more than one**.

✓ to show whether the **plural** of each word is made by adding **-s** or **-es**. One has been done for you.

	-s	-es
chair	✓	
book		
wish		

G 1 mark

/ 4
Total for this page

40   © Rising Stars UK Ltd 2014   *You may photocopy this page*

5 Match each sentence with the correct punctuation.
One has been done for you.

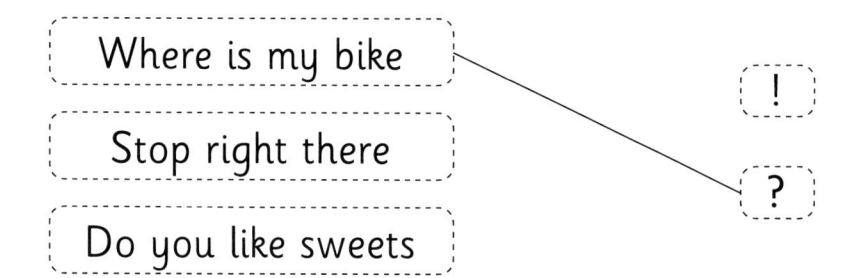

- Where is my bike
- Stop right there
- Do you like sweets

- !
- ?

(Where is my bike — ?)

P
1 mark

6 Which word would fit into **both** of these sentences?
Circle **one** word.

the   and   to

My cat is black _____ white.

I went to the park _____ played football.

G
1 mark

7 Write **-ing**, **-ed** or **-er** in each space.
One has been done for you.

-ing   -ed   -er

I like help**ing** my grandad.

This is my favourite red jump_____.

We play_____ football yesterday.

V
1 mark

/3
Total for this page

8 Match each singular word with the plural.

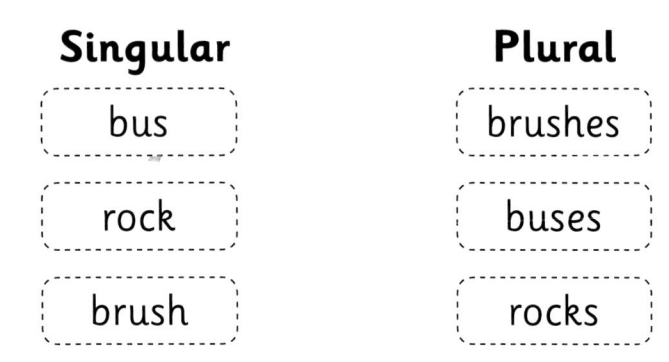

Singular	Plural
bus	brushes
rock	buses
brush	rocks

G
1 mark

9 Look at this sentence. There are **two** mistakes.
Copy out the sentence and correct the mistakes.

i played with my friends today

_____

_____

P
1 mark

10 Match the different ways of writing each word.
One has been done for you.

cannot — wasn't
do not — can't
was not — don't

(line drawn from "was not" to "wasn't")

P
1 mark

/ 10
Total for this test

Year 1 Spelling: Spring test 2: *Teacher's script*

This test should take approximately ten minutes to complete. Tell the children that on their answer sheet there are ten pictures. You are going to read out the word for each picture. Tell the children to listen carefully to the word and write it next to the picture, making sure they spell it correctly. Read out each word in turn to the children as below, repeating each word three times. At the end of the test read out all ten words again. Follow the script below when administering the test.

1. **Spelling one:** the word is **cats**.
   (the word is) **cats**
   (the word is) **cats**

2. **Spelling two:** the word is **house**.
   (the word is) **house**
   (the word is) **house**

3. **Spelling three:** the word is **his**.
   (the word is) **his**
   (the word is) **his**

4. **Spelling four:** the word is **jumping**.
   (the word is) **jumping**
   (the word is) **jumping**

5. **Spelling five:** the word is **me**.
   (the word is) **me**
   (the word is) **me**

6. **Spelling six:** the word is **rabbit**.
   (the word is) **rabbit**
   (the word is) **rabbit**

7. **Spelling seven:** the word is **love**.
   (the word is) **love**
   (the word is) **love**

8. **Spelling eight:** the word is **tree**.
   (the word is) **tree**
   (the word is) **tree**

9. **Spelling nine:** the word is **park**.
   (the word is) **park**
   (the word is) **park**

10. **Spelling ten:** the word is **one**.
    (the word is) **one**
    (the word is) **one**

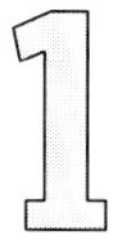

© Rising Stars UK Ltd 2014   *You may photocopy this page*

Year 1 *Spelling: Spring test 2*

Name:	Class:	Date:

Your teacher will tell you the word for each picture.
Write the word in the space.

1. _____

2. _____

3. _____

4. _____

5. _____

1 mark

1 mark

1 mark

1 mark

1 mark

/ 5

Total for this page

Year 1   *Spelling: Spring test 2*

6)   _____   1 mark

7)   _____   1 mark

8)   _____   1 mark

9)   _____   1 mark

10) _____   1 mark

/ 10
Total for this test

Year 1 Spelling: Summer test 1: *Teacher's script*

This test should take approximately ten minutes to complete. Tell the children you are going to read out ten sentences to them. Each sentence has a word missing on their answer sheet. Tell the children to listen carefully to the missing word and fill it in, making sure they spell it correctly. You will read the word, then the word within a sentence, then repeat the word a third time. Now read out each sentence to the children as below. At the end of the test read out all ten sentences again. Follow the script below when administering the test.

NB: You may like to carry out this test in small groups initially, as children may need guidance to put their finger in the empty space while you read the sentence.

1 **Spelling one:** the word is **pie**.
Ben loved apple **pie**.
The word is **pie**.

2 **Spelling two:** the word is **has**.
That house **has** a red door.
The word is **has**.

3 **Spelling three:** the word is **my**.
I went to see **my** friend.
The word is **my**.

4 **Spelling four:** the word is **down**.
The children sat **down** on the carpet.
The word is **down**.

5 **Spelling five:** the word is **some**.
Please could I have **some** more?
The word is **some**.

6 **Spelling six:** the word is **light**.
Mum turned on the **light**.
The word is **light**.

7 **Spelling seven:** the word is **do**.
What **do** you want to eat?
The word is **do**.

8 **Spelling eight:** the word is **road**.
Penny crossed the **road** with her dad.
The word is **road**.

9 **Spelling nine:** the word is **like**.
The boy did not **like** the dark.
The word is **like**.

10 **Spelling ten:** the word is **they**.
After school, **they** played outside.
The word is **they**.

Year 1   Spelling: Summer test 1

Name:	Class:	Date:

Your teacher will tell you each missing word.
Write the word in the space.

1) Ben loved apple _____ .

1 mark

2) That house _____ a red door.

1 mark

3) I went to see _____ friend.

1 mark

4) The children sat _____ on the carpet.

1 mark

5) Please could I have _____ more?

1 mark

/ 5

Total for this page

Rising Stars UK Ltd 2014   You may photocopy this page   47

Year 1   *Spelling: Summer test 1*

6) Mum turned on the _____.

7) What _____ you want to eat?

8) Penny crossed the _____ with her dad.

9) The boy did not _____ the dark.

10) After school, _____ played outside.

Year 1   Spelling: Summer test 2: *Teacher's script*

This test should take approximately ten minutes to complete. Tell the children you are going to read out ten sentences to them. Each sentence has a word missing on their answer sheet. Tell the children to listen carefully to the missing word and fill it in, making sure they spell it correctly. You will read the word, then the word within a sentence, then repeat the word a third time. Now read out each question to the children as below. At the end of the test read out all ten sentences again. Follow the script below when administering the test.

1. **Spelling one:** the word is **you**.
I am going to catch **you**!
The word is **you**.

2. **Spelling two:** the word is **happy**.
My dog is always **happy**.
The word is **happy**.

3. **Spelling three:** the word is **said**.
Dad **said** he loved the present.
The word is **said**.

4. **Spelling four:** the word is **rain**.
The children splashed in the **rain**.
The word is **rain**.

5. **Spelling five:** the word is **our**.
This is **our** house.
The word is **our**.

6. **Spelling six:** the word is **more**.
Sam asked for **more** carrots.
The word is **more**.

7. **Spelling seven:** the word is **grow**.
A sunflower can **grow** very tall.
The word is **grow**.

8. **Spelling eight:** the word is **were**.
The two boys **were** very excited.
The word is **were**.

9. **Spelling nine:** the word is **about**.
The story was **about** a naughty mouse.
The word is **about**.

10. **Spelling ten:** the word is **where**.
Where shall we go next?
The word is **where**.

Year 1   *Spelling: Summer test 2*

Name:	Class:	Date:

Your teacher will tell you each missing word.
Write the word in the space.

(1)   I am going to catch _____ !

(2)   My dog is always _____ .

(3)   Dad _____ he loved the present.

(4)   The children splashed in the _____ .

(5)   This is _____ house.

Year 1   *Spelling: Summer test 2*

6) Sam asked for _____ carrots.

7) A sunflower can _____ very tall.

8) The two boys _____ very excited.

9) The story was _____ a naughty mouse.

10) _____ shall we go next?

Answers and mark schemes
Reading: Autumn test 1: Fiction

	Autumn test 1: Fiction	AF	Mark
1	[cat] ✓	1	1
2	[leg] ✓	1	1
3	[vet] ✓	1	1
4	dog ✓	2	1
5	sad ✓	2	1
6	The cat is Sam's pet. yes ✓	2	1
7	The cat bit a dog's leg. no ✓	2	1
8	The cat's leg hurts. yes ✓	2	1
9	The vet was sad. no ✓	2	1
10	The leg will get better. yes ✓	2	1

Reading: Autumn test 2: Non-fiction

	Autumn test 2: Non-fiction	AF	Mark
1	cat → hamster	1	1
2	hamster → bird	1	1
3	bird → cat	1	1
4	vet ✓	2	1
5	pets ✓	2	1
6	Tess helps vets. no ✓	2	1
7	A cat is a pet. yes ✓	2	1
8	A hamster is a pet. yes ✓	2	1
9	Tess is hurt. no ✓	2	1
10	You can take a pet to see the vet. yes ✓	2	1

Reading: Spring test 1: Fiction

	Spring test 1: Fiction	AF	Mark
1	[cat image] ✓	1	1
2	thin ✓	2	1
3	food ✓	2	1
4	ate ✓	2	1
5	fat ✓	2	1
6	The cat was in the park. yes ✓	2	1
7	Max gave the cat to the dog. no ✓	2	1
8	The cat ate a bowl of food. yes ✓	2	1
9	Max fed the fish every day. no ✓	2	1
10	Mum fed the cat. no ✓	2	1

Reading: Spring test 2: Non-fiction

	Spring test 2: Non-fiction	AF	Mark	Extra information
1	[tin of cat food image] — This is a tin of cat food.	1	1	Award 1 mark for the correct match.
2	fish ✓	1	1	
3	cat ✓	1	1	
4	tank ✓	2	1	
5	weeds ✓	2	1	
6	You must feed a cat every day. yes ✓	2	1	
7	You must feed a fish every week. yes ✓	2	1	
8	Cats need water. yes ✓	2	1	
9	Fish eat cat food. no ✓	2	1	
10	Can a fish eat weeds? yes ✓	2	1	

Reading: Summer test 1: Fiction

	Summer test 1: Fiction	AF	Mark	Extra information
1	(horse image) ✓	1	1	
2	farm ✓	2	1	
3	help ✓	2	1	
4	mud ✓	2	1	
5	grass ✓	2	1	
6	Sam gets the eggs and the logs. yes ✓	2	1	
7	Washing the tractor is easy. no ✓	3	1	
8	At the end, Sam and Mop are happy. yes ✓	3	1	
9	Award 1 mark for answers that refer to Sam and Mop wanting to play in the mud, e.g.: • *They want to play in the mud.* Also allow answers that refer to the fact that they can't play in the mud because they have to help Dad, e.g.: • *Sam's dad wants/needs help.* • *They have to help Dad (first).*	3	1	Do not allow answers that are not text based or that repeat the questions, e.g.: *because they were upset.* Do not penalise incorrect grammar, spelling or punctuation.
10	Award 1 mark for answers that refer to Sam and Mop having finished their jobs for Dad, e.g.: • *They have done the jobs.* • *They have helped Dad.*	3	1	Do not allow answers that are not text based or that repeat the questions, e.g.: *because they like playing in the mud.* Do not penalise incorrect grammar, spelling or punctuation

Reading: Summer test 2: Non-fiction

	Summer test 2: Non-fiction			AF	Mark	Extra information
		something you need	a rule	2	2	Award 1 mark for each correctly ticked.
	armbands	✓				
1	Stay with Mum or Dad.		✓			
2	swimming costume	✓				
3	trunks ✓			2	1	
4	safe ✓			2	1	
5	pool ✓			2	1	
6	You can jump into the pool. no ✓			2	1	
7	Playing in the water can be fun. yes ✓			2	1	
8	You can go in the water on your own. no ✓			2	1	
9	Award 1 mark for answers that refer to the fact that you might slip.			2	1	Do not allow answers that are not text based or that repeat the question, e.g.: *your dad will run after you.* Do not penalise incorrect grammar, spelling or punctuation.
10	Award 1 mark for answers that refer to the fact that you might hurt another person.			2	1	Do not allow answers that are not text based or that repeat the question, e.g.: *because the lifeguard said.* Do not penalise incorrect grammar, spelling or punctuation.

Grammar, punctuation and vocabulary: Autumn test 1

	Autumn test 1	G, P, V	Mark
1	sun, sock	S	1
2	mouse, man	S	1
3	cat, hat	S	1
4	dog	G	1
5	hen	G	1
6	pin	G	1
7	was	G	1
8	in	G	1
9	like	G	1
10	the	G	1

Grammar, punctuation and vocabulary: Autumn test 2

	Autumn test 2	G, P, V	Mark
1	s	S	1
2	sh	S	1
3	hat	G	1
4	bed	G	1
5	tap	G	1
6	my	G	1
7	you	G	1
8	going	G	1
9	like	G	1
10	grab	G	1

Grammar, punctuation and vocabulary: Spring test 1

	Spring test 1	G, P, V	Mark
1	m	S	1
2	bus	G	1
3	zip	G	1
4	frog	G	1
5	fish	G	1
6	is	G	1
7	going	G	1
8	have	G	1
9	house	G	1
10	make	G	1

Grammar, punctuation and vocabulary: Spring test 2

	Spring test 2	G, P, V	Mark	Extra information
1	lower case letter → capital letter b → E e → R n → B (given) r → N	P	1	Award 1 mark for all correctly matched.
2	frogs, boys	G	1	Award 1 mark for both words (and no others) circled. Also accept other ways of indicating answers, e.g. ticking.
3	Who is that? ✓	P	1	
4	My hat is red.	G	1	
5	kind	V	1	Award 1 mark for the correct word matched with un- (and no other lines drawn).
6	cars, dogs	G	1	Award 1 mark for both correct.
7	buzzing ✓	V	1	
8	james	P	1	Award 1 mark for the correct word (and no others) circled. Also accept other ways of indicating answers, e.g. ticking or clearly changing the correct letter into a capital.
9	Award 1 mark for an appropriate, grammatically correct question beginning with *What*, e.g.: • What is your name? • What is that? • What shall we play?	G	1	Do not penalise incorrect spelling.
10	Award 1 mark for an appropriate, grammatically correct sentence that begins with a capital letter and has correct end punctuation, e.g.: • He is eating the apple. • The boy eats an apple. • He likes apples. • The boy is happy and full up. • The boy has an apple and he is chewing.	G	1	Sentences must be relevant to the picture; they may comment on the boy/apple or may refer to the boy's feelings. Do not penalise answers that add detail not in the picture, e.g.: a red apple. Sentences are most likely to be simple but may be compound or complex. Do not penalise incorrect spelling.

Grammar, punctuation and vocabulary: Summer test 1

	Summer test 1	G, P, V	Mark	Extra information
1	faster	V	1	
2	fox, cat	G	1	Award 1 mark for both correct.
3	She has a green coat. ✓	G	1	
4	Come back	P	1	Award 1 mark for the correct sentence matched with (!) (and no other lines drawn).
5	It was windy _____ cold. ✓	G	1	Also accept other ways of indicating answer, e.g. clearly writing *and* in the space for this sentence (and not writing it in any of the others).
6	Tim had a pet fish.	G	1	
7	boat*s*	G	1	
8	fair, happy	V	1	Award 1 mark for both correct.
9	Award 1 mark for an appropriate, grammatically correct sentence beginning with *I*, which has correct end punctuation, e.g.: • *I have blue eyes.* • *I don't like carrots.* • *I am six.*	G	1	Do not penalise incorrect spelling.

10	Original sentence:
	   On friday I went to the park.
	Corrected sentence:
	   On Friday I went to the park.
		P	1	

Grammar, punctuation and vocabulary: Summer test 2

	Summer test 2	G, P, V	Mark	Extra information
1	Award 1 mark for two appropriate words, e.g.: spotty/spiky/happy/smiling/hairy/fat, etc.	G	1	Children must insert two different words.
2	tallest	V	1	
3	Award 1 mark for an appropriate, grammatically correct question beginning with *Why*, punctuated at the end with a question mark, e.g.: • *Why is the sky blue?* • *Why can birds fly?* • *Why are you being silly?*	G	1	Do not penalise incorrect spelling.
4	**chair** (given): -s ✓ book: -s ✓ wish: -es ✓	G	1	Award 1 mark for both ticks correct (and none incorrect). Use of crosses to indicate answers is also acceptable.
5	Where is my bike (given) — ? Stop right there — ! Do you like sweets — ?	P	1	Award 1 mark for both correct.
6	and	G	1	Award 1 mark for the correct word circled.
7	helping (given) jump**er** play**ed**	V	1	Award 1 mark for both correct.
8	**Singular — Plural** bus — buses rock — rocks brush — brushes	G	1	Award 1 mark for all correctly matched.

9	Original sentence:
	  i played with my friends today
	Corrected sentence:
	  (I) played with my friends today(.)
		P	1	Award 1 mark for both mistakes corrected (and no other mistakes introduced, e.g. an incorrect capital letter on friends).
				
				Do not penalise minor spelling errors such as playd instead of played.

10	cannot — can't do not — don't was not (given) — wasn't	P	1	Award 1 mark for all correctly matched.

Coverage grid: Reading

Test	Question	AF	Strand*	Marks
Autumn test 1 (fiction)	1	1	N/A	1
	2	1	N/A	1
	3	1	N/A	1
	4	2	Comprehension	1
	5	2	Comprehension	1
	6	2	Comprehension	1
	7	2	Comprehension	1
	8	2	Comprehension	1
	9	2	Comprehension	1
	10	2	Comprehension	1
Autumn test 2 (non-fiction)	1	1	N/A	1
	2	1	N/A	1
	3	1	N/A	1
	4	2	Comprehension	1
	5	2	Comprehension	1
	6	2	Comprehension	1
	7	2	Comprehension	1
	8	2	Comprehension	1
	9	2	Comprehension	1
	10	2	Comprehension	1
Spring test 1 (fiction)	1	1	N/A	1
	2	2	Comprehension	1
	3	2	Comprehension	1
	4	2	Comprehension	1
	5	2	Comprehension	1
	6	2	Comprehension	1
	7	2	Comprehension	1
	8	2	Comprehension	1
	9	2	Comprehension	1
	10	2	Comprehension	1

© Rising Stars UK Ltd 2014   *You may photocopy this page*

Year 1 *Coverage grid: Reading*

Test	Question	AF	Strand*	Marks
Spring test 2 (non-fiction)	1	1	N/A	1
	2	1	N/A	1
	3	1	N/A	1
	4	2	Comprehension	1
	5	2	Comprehension	1
	6	2	Comprehension	1
	7	2	Comprehension	1
	8	2	Comprehension	1
	9	2	Comprehension	1
	10	2	Comprehension	1
Summer test 1 (fiction)	1	1	N/A	1
	2	2	Comprehension	1
	3	2	Comprehension	1
	4	2	Comprehension	1
	5	2	Comprehension	1
	6	2	Comprehension	1
	7	3	Making inferences	1
	8	3	Making inferences	1
	9	3	Making inferences	1
	10	3	Making inferences	1
Summer test 2 (non-fiction)	1	2	Comprehension	1
	2	2	Comprehension	1
	3	2	Comprehension	1
	4	2	Comprehension	1
	5	2	Comprehension	1
	6	2	Comprehension	1
	7	2	Comprehension	1
	8	2	Comprehension	1
	9	2	Comprehension	1
	10	2	Comprehension	1

* From 2016 AFs will be replaced by strands in national tests.

Coverage grid: Grammar, punctuation and vocabulary

Note: content is listed using the STA test framework wording. 'Spelling' in Year 1 is the exception as these are actually Reception-level questions and therefore pre-National Curriculum.

Test	Content	Number of questions
Autumn 1	Spelling	3
	Nouns	3
	Verbs	2
	Prepositions	1
	Determiners	1
Autumn 2	Spelling	2
	Nouns	3
	Possessive pronouns	1
	Pronouns	1
	Present and past progressive continuous	1
	Verbs	1
Spring 1	Spelling	1
	Nouns	4
	Verbs	3
	Present and past progressive continuous	1
	Pronouns	1
Spring 2	Capital letters	2
	Subject–verb agreement	2
	Question marks	1
	Sentences	2
	Prefixes	1
	Suffixes	1
	Questions	1

Year 1 *Coverage grid: Grammar, punctuation and vocabulary*

Summer 1	Suffixes	1
	Subject–verb agreement	2
	Statements	1
	Exclamation marks	1
	Co-ordinating conjunctions	1
	Sentences	2
	Prefixes	1
	Capital letters	1
Summer 2	Adjectives	1
	Suffixes	2
	Questions	1
	Subject–verb agreement	2
	Exclamation marks/Questions	1
	Sentences	1
	Capital letters/Full stops	1
	Apostrophes	1